BIRCH
BOOKS

First published by Birch Books 2020

ISBN (978-93-90787-03-6)

Email : books.birch@gmail.com

Pause please, Miss Porcupine.

Ruchira Darda

For my sons Aryaveer and Adhiraj and

my teacher Anila Vijay,

who simply taught me to PAUSE!

Wherever I go,
Whoever I meet,
They shy away,
Before they greet.

If they say something,
And I disagree,
A chill runs down my spine.
They all shout together,
Pause please, Miss Porcupine.

Last time I met the cheetah,

He came too close.

I assumed he would attack,

And then time froze.

My quills penetrated through his feet,
Before he could speak he was beat.
And everyone squealed together,
Pause please, Miss Porcupine.

I didn't mean to hurt him,
I didn't say a word.
But these darn quills,
know not better, shot out like a bird.

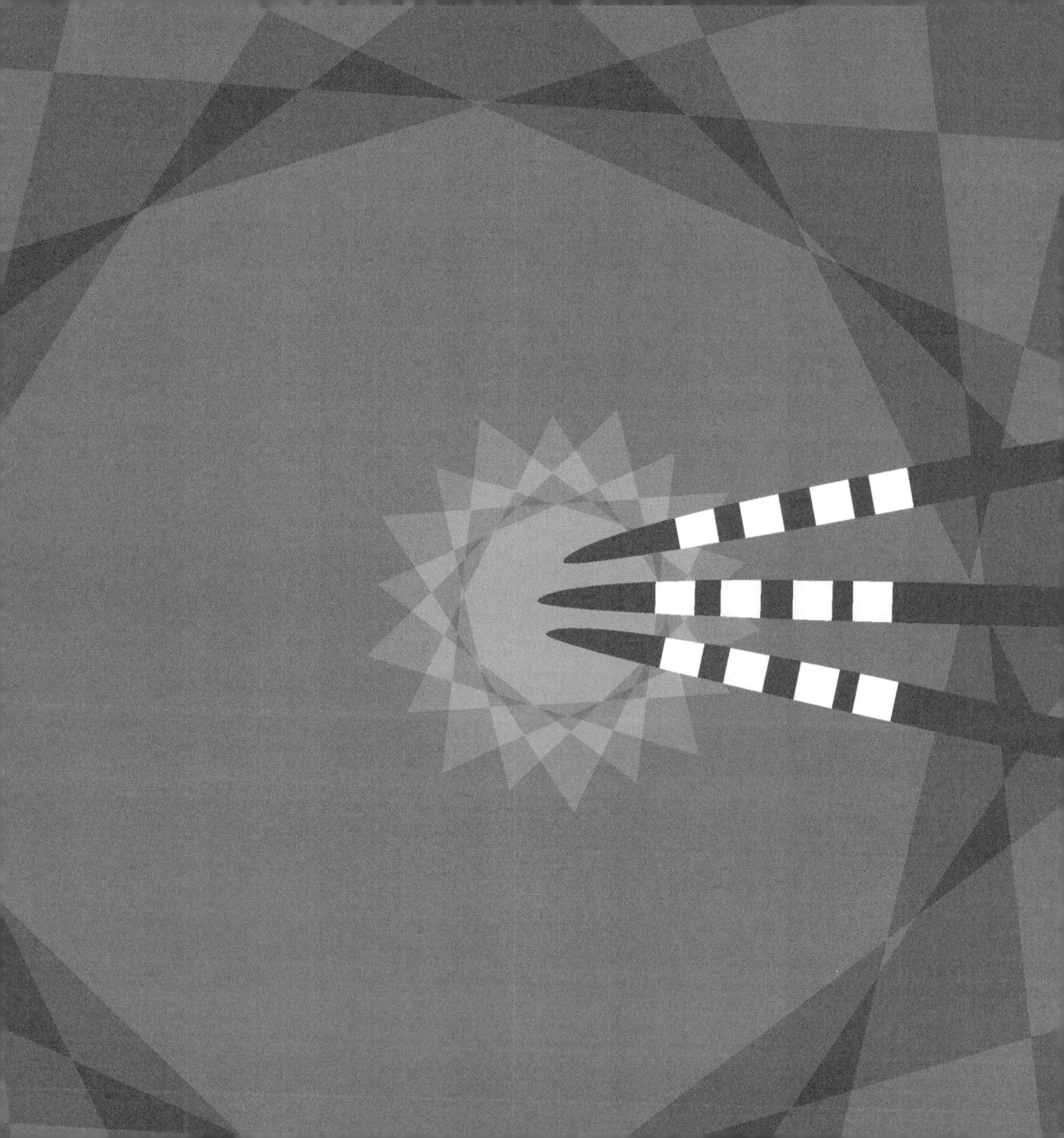

If I tell you,

Promise you won't tell another.

The other day,

I pierced my own mother.

Oh how miserable, I was.

For my Mum came to love,

And out came my claws!

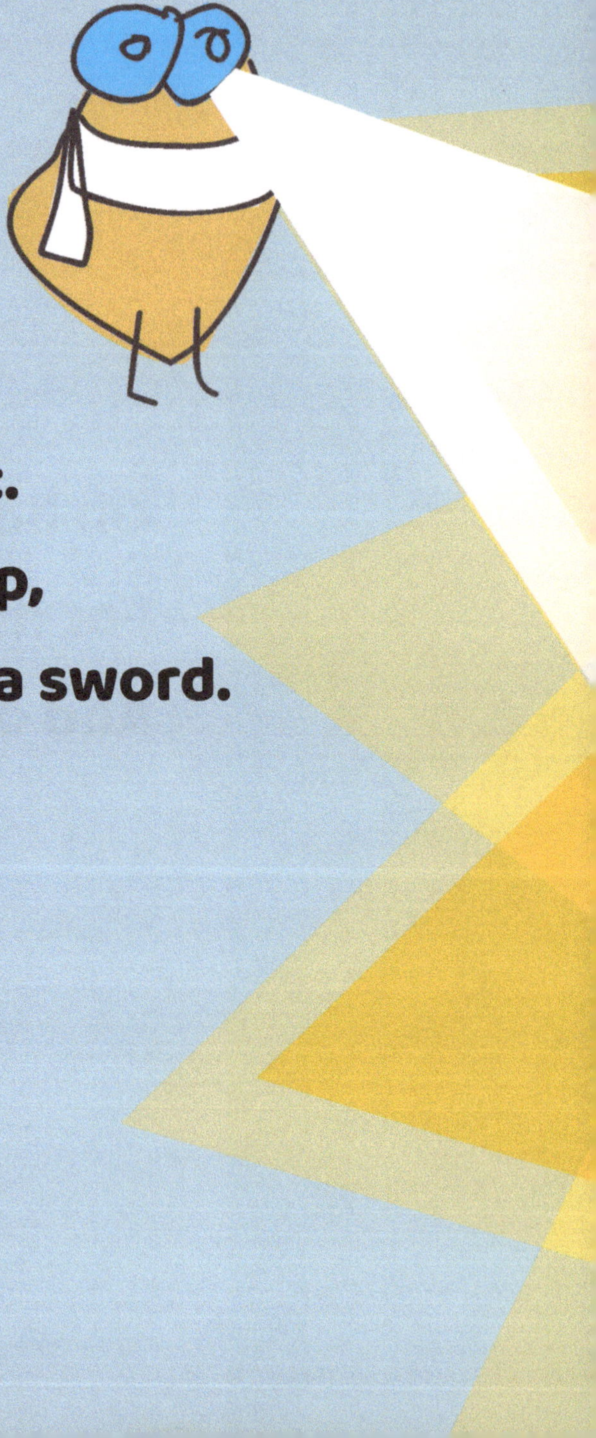

The wise old owl,
Has shared a thought.
Breathe nice and deep,
Before you draw out a sword.

And let their voices echo in thine,
Pause please, Miss Porcupine.

- - -×- - -×- - -×- - -

Miss Porcupine has been practicing to pause.

Why don't you practice with her?

Breathe in nice and deep

1...2...3...

Breathe out.

Phew!

Let's do this once more...

See how many
new friends
Miss Porcupine has made!
Just because she
learnt to pause!

Miss Porcupine's new friends!

The cheeky monkey
The wise owl
The cheerful cheetah
The happy hare
The loving Llama

ABOUT THE AUTHOR

Ruchira Darda is a parent to two inspiring young children. They spend time together weaving stories and exploring the world through them.

Ruchira has a decade of experience working with children via her children's enrichment centre - The Yellow Door. Her pursuit of spirituality is the purpose behind her storytelling. She is an expert on personalities and is a sought after Relationship and Parenting Coach. Her quest for spirituality coupled with her experience with women and children has led her to simplfying her learnings for children.

While she believes spiritual learning should come to children from a young age she also believes that everything we say to our children doesn't need to be so structured. That's why her storytelling is a blend of spurts of laughter, tamed with a dose of goodness.